T0413753

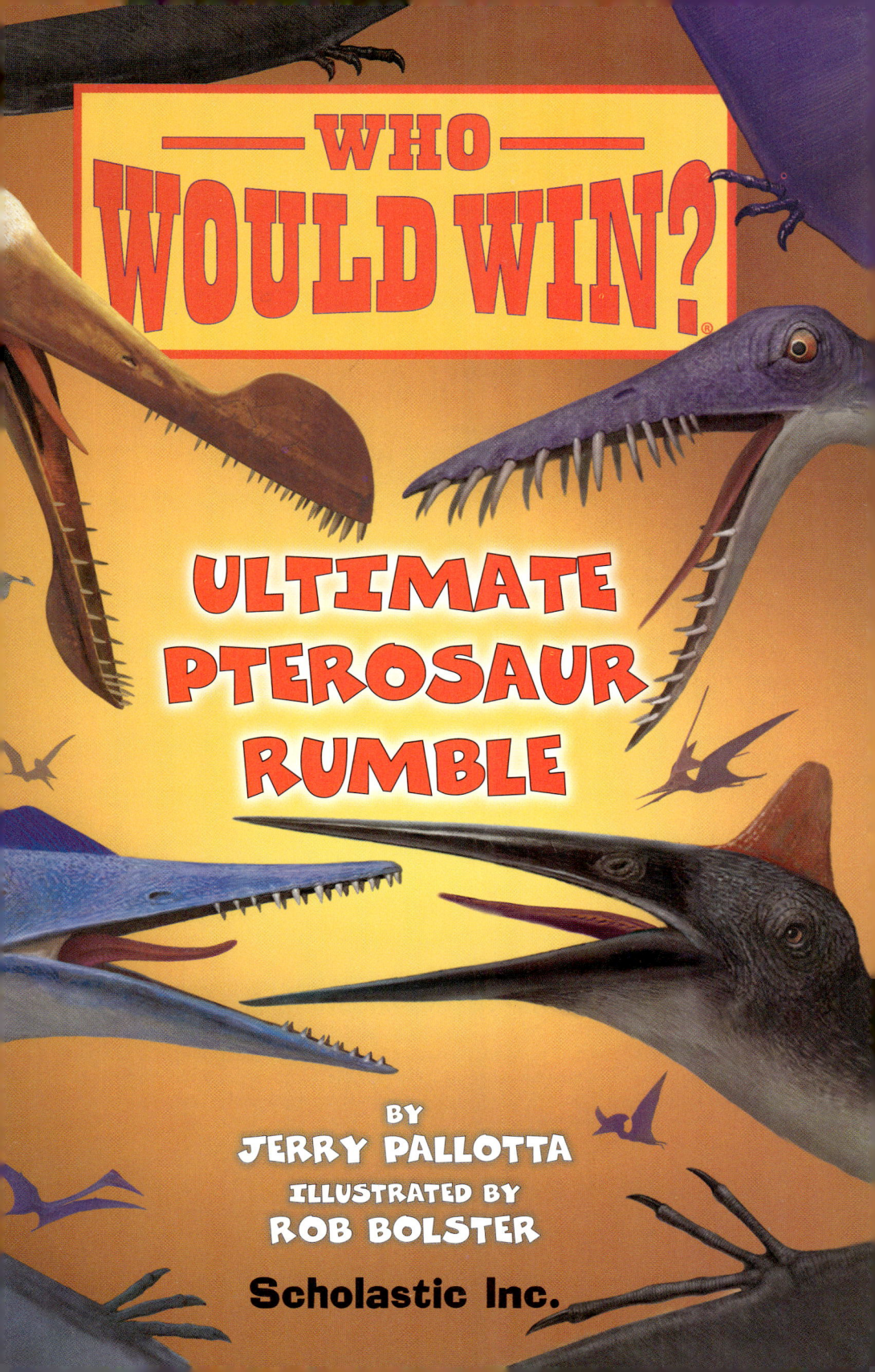

WHO WOULD WIN?

ULTIMATE PTEROSAUR RUMBLE

BY
JERRY PALLOTTA

ILLUSTRATED BY
ROB BOLSTER

Scholastic Inc.

16 PTEROSAURS BRACKET

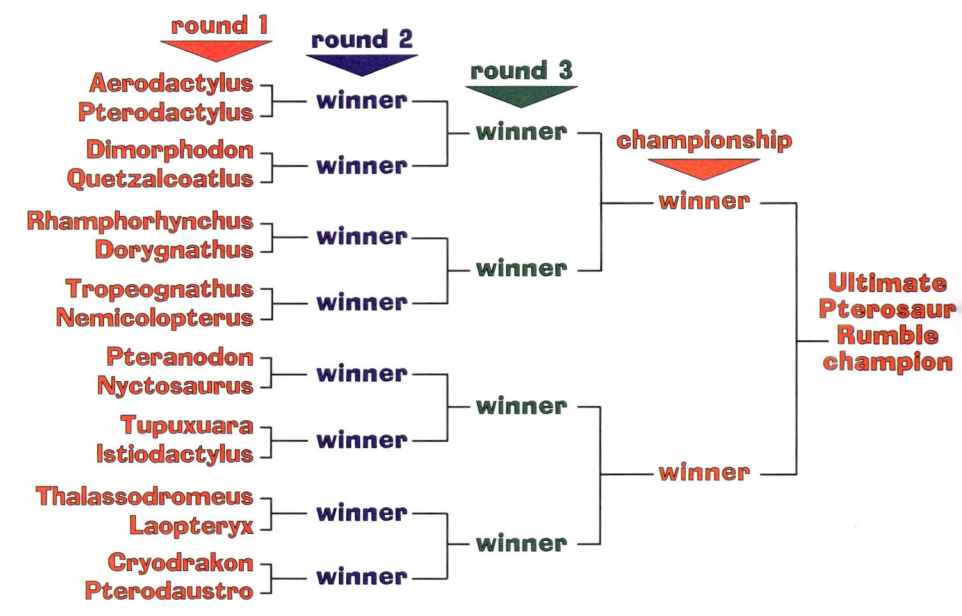

Hello to my school-visit author road buddies: Jack Gantos, Ralph Masiello, Roland Smith, Pam Muñoz Ryan, Brod Bagert, Mike Artell, Michael Shoulders, E.B. Lewis, David Biedrzycki, Shelley Gill, Barbara McGrath, Floyd Cooper, and Steve Swinburne. Together we have gone on thousands of school visits, helping children to read.
—J.P.

Thank you to all the paleontologists who dug deep to discover those wonderful fossils.
—R.B.

Text copyright © 2025 by Jerry Pallotta.
Illustrations copyright © 2025 by Rob Bolster.

Library of Congress Cataloging-in-Publication Data available
ISBN 978-1-339-00095-4

10 9 8 7 6 5 4 3   25 26 27 28 29
Printed in the U.S.A.   40
First printing, 2025

The creatures in this book are called pterosaurs. Pterosaurs were flying reptiles. They are extinct.

Sixteen pterosaurs meet for a bracketed battle. If a pterosaur loses a fight, it is out of the competition. May the best, most athletic pterosaur win!

Aerodactylus and other pterosaurs had two legs. An Aerodactylus's feet were not able to pick up food.

"AIR-OH-DAK-TIL-US"
AERODACTYLUS VS. PTERODACTYLUS
"TER-UH-DAK-TIL-US"

ROUND 1 — MATCH 1

This Pterodactylus just flew into an area where another pterosaur lives. Uh-oh!

FACT
Pterosaurs were not dinosaurs.

Insects were probably the first creatures to fly. Pterosaur were the first vertebrate animals to fly.

The Aerodactylus notices the Pterodactylus and flies toward it. The Pterodactylus dodges the Aerodactylus. The Aerodactylus is forced to crash.

NAME FACT
Pterodactylus *means "winged finger."*

BONE FACT
Vertebrates are animals with spines.

PTERODACTYLUS WINS!

Their names are challenging. Sound them out!

The Dimorphodon was a medium-sized pterosaur. It had two different types of teeth—long and short. It is looking forward to biting the Quetzalcoatlus.

"DYE-MOR-FO-DON"

DIMORPHODON VS. QUETZALCOATLUS

"KET-ZEL-KWAT-A-LUS"

Quetzalcoatlus was the largest pterosaur that ever lived. It was the size of a fighter jet. Maybe someday the fossil of a larger one will be found. Will you be the scientist who discovers it?

The Quetzalcoatlus is huge. It flies right at the Dimorphodon. One bite! Crunch! Big defeats small.

DID YOU KNOW?
Pterosaurs were not birds.

QUETZALCOATLUS WINS!

THINK
Do you think that pterosaurs flew in a V formation like modern-day birds do? How would we ever know?

Some people think pterosaurs looked like bats. Bat wings have five fingers. Pterosaurs had four fingers.

The name Rhamphorhynchus means "beaked nose." It had a long, strange tail. Scientists think it might have controlled its flight by moving its tail.

"RAM-FUH-RING-KUS"

RHAMPHORHYNCHUS VS. DORYGNATHUS

"DOR-IG-NAH-THUS"

ROUND 1

MATCH 3

We think Dorygnathus was a fish eater. It lived near the ocean. Pterosaurs lived millions of years ago. How could we know what they ate? We look for clues!

NAME FACT
A dory is a wooden work boat.

The Rhamphorhynchus sneaks up on the Dorygnathus while it is hunting for fish. The Rhamphorhynchus decide to be aggressive. It smashes into the Dorygnathus.

The Dorygnathus is in trouble. Rhamphorhynchus's shar teeth finish the job.

RHAMPHORHYNCHUS WINS!

The name Tropeognathus means "keel jaw." Its head was shaped like the keel of a boat. Tropeognathus was larger than the average pterosaur. It could have a 28-foot wingspan.

ROUND 1 TROPEOGNATHUS VS. NEMICOLOPTERUS MATCH 4

"NEH·ME·CO·LOP·TER·US"

The Nemicolopterus is the smallest known pterosaur. A human could hold one in their hand. Nemicolopterus lived millions and millions years before humans. Nemicolopterus probably ate insects and small worms.

This matchup is not fair. Huge versus tiny!

It will be a quick battle. The Tropeognathus flies over the Nemicolopterus. Is the Nemicolopterus shifty and sneaky? It doesn't matter. Gulp! The Tropeognathus swallows it.

TROPEOGNATHUS WINS!

We can only wonder what pterosaurs tasted like. If Tropeognathus lived today, it could swoop down and capture you on your way to school. Yikes!

A Pteranodon's head looked too long for its body. When a Pteranodon flew, it steered with its wings, tail, legs, and the crest on its head.

DEFINITION
Crests were part of a creature's skull. They were usually located between the eyes. Pterosaurs had many differently shaped crests.

"TER-AN-O-DON"

PTERANODON VS. NYCTOSAURUS

"NIC-TOE-SOR-US"

ROUND 1

MATCH 5

The Nyctosaurus had a very unusual crest on its head. It might have been the strangest head of all. It may have looked like a sail on a sailboat.

THINK!
Could the Nyctosaurus's crest protect it from being attacked from above?

The Pteranodon flies over and bites the crest of the Nyctosaurus. It doesn't hurt the Nyctosaurus. The Pteranodon doesn't let go. It hangs on and on.

The Pteranodon wears the Nyctosaurus out. The Nyctosaurus has to land to catch its breath. The Pteranodon moves in and eats it!

PTERANODON WINS!

Tupuxuara was a toothless pterosaur.

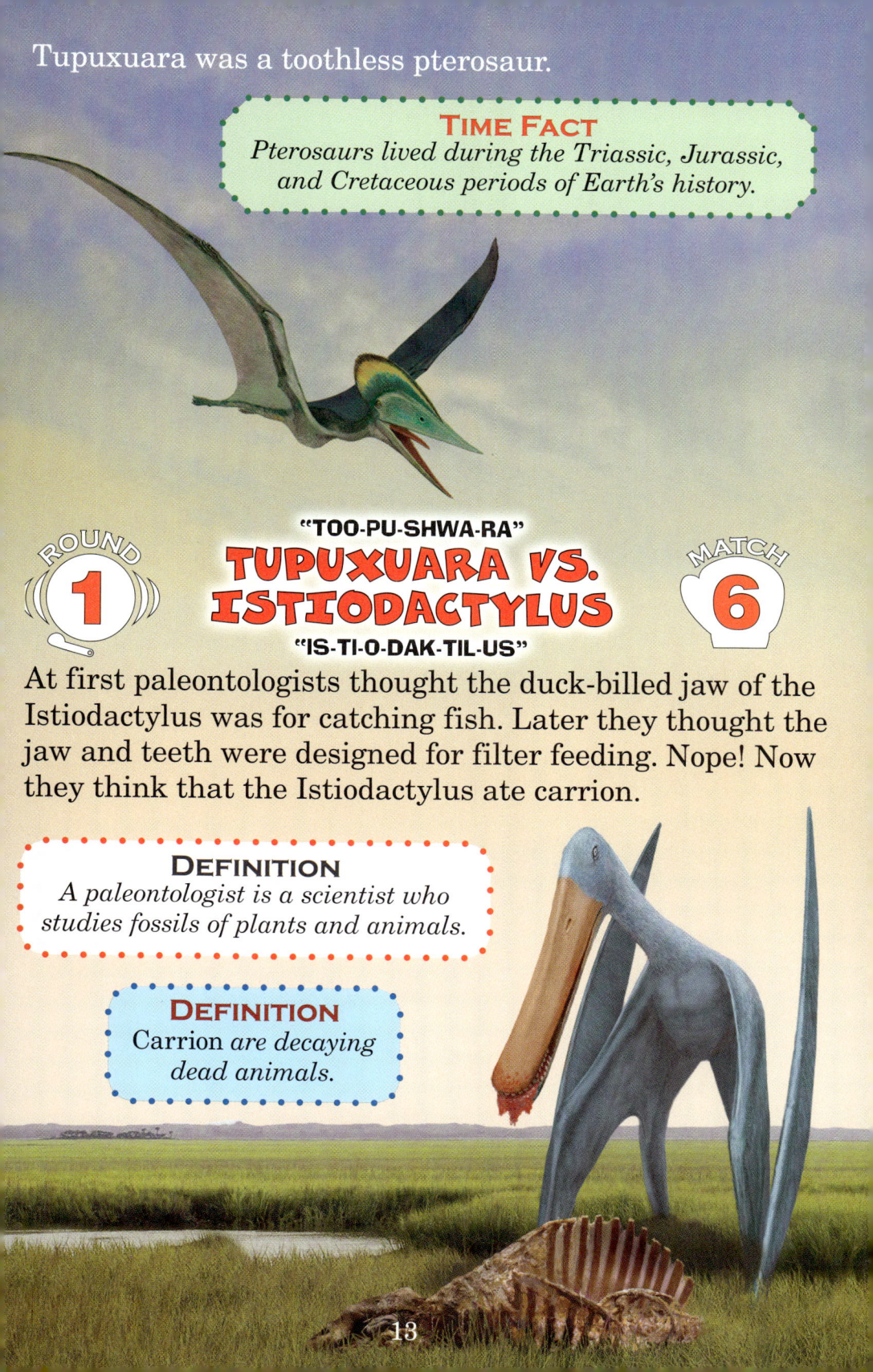

ROUND 1

TIME FACT
Pterosaurs lived during the Triassic, Jurassic, and Cretaceous periods of Earth's history.

"TOO-PU-SHWA-RA"

TUPUXUARA VS. ISTIODACTYLUS

"IS-TI-O-DAK-TIL-US"

MATCH 6

At first paleontologists thought the duck-billed jaw of the Istiodactylus was for catching fish. Later they thought the jaw and teeth were designed for filter feeding. Nope! Now they think that the Istiodactylus ate carrion.

DEFINITION
A paleontologist is a scientist who studies fossils of plants and animals.

DEFINITION
Carrion are decaying dead animals.

The Tupuxuara uses its pointed head to poke the Istiodactylus. It causes minor cuts.

The Istiodactylus quickly turns on the Tupuxuara and forces it to the ground. The Tupuxuara breaks a bone in one of its wings. It breaks a leg also. Uh-oh! There are hungry velociraptors nearby!

NAME FACT
Istiodactylus means "sail finger."

ISTIODACTYLUS WINS!

Thalassodromeus was above average in size. Its long name means "sea runner." Like other pterosaurs, the Thalassodromeus's eyes were on both sides of its head. Pterosaurs had what's called monocular vision. That means each eye looks in a different direction.

"THE-LASS-A-DRO-ME-US"

THALASSODROMEUS VS. LAOPTERYX

"LEE-OP-TER-IKS"

Laopteryx fossils are very rare. They were originally thought to belong to a bird. Then the fossils were thought to be a dinosaur. Scientists eventually realized they were pterosaur fossils.

HISTORY FACT
The Laopteryx fossil was named by famous dinosaur hunter Othniel Marsh.

The Thalassodromeus has a 15-foot wingspan. It is much bigger than the Laopteryx. This is not a fair match.

The Laopteryx tries to avoid the Thalassodromeus. The Laopteryx gets tired. The Thalassodromeus overpowers it. Sorry, Laopteryx!

THALASSODROMEUS WINS!

The Cryodrakon may have been a cousin to the Quetzalcoatlus. Paleontologists think it had a 30-foot wingspan. Cryodrakon was a huge creature. It was larger than any known bird today.

COOL NAME
The name Cryodrakon means "cold dragon."

ROUND 1

"CRY-OH-DRAH-KON"
CRYODRAKON VS. PTERODAUSTRO
"TER-UH-DOW-STRO"

MATCH 8

The Pterodaustro was only one-third the size of the Cryodrakon. The Pterodaustro had rounded jaws with a mouth full of brush-like teeth. Its teeth were perfect for filter feeding on creatures from the ocean. Maybe its strange mouth was also good for capturing large amounts of bugs!

Cryodrakon is just too large for the Pterodaustro. The Cryodrakon circles and circles and circles. It eventually corners the smaller Pterodaustro. The Pterodaustro's fancy mouth is of no help in a battle against such a huge pterosaur.

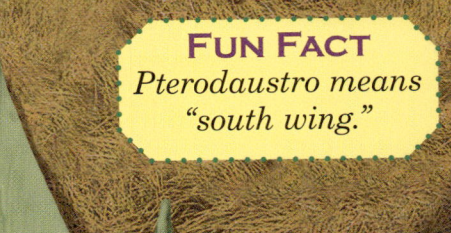

FUN FACT
Pterodaustro means "south wing."

CRYODRAKON WINS!

On to the second round. Only eight pterosaurs are left in the competition. In sports they call it the "Elite Eight." We will call it the Pterosaur Eight!

No one really knows what color the pterosaurs were. On Earth today, lizards, birds, fish, frogs, snakes, butterflies, crabs, and flowers come in all different colors. It is only logical that pterosaurs did too! We know about pterosaurs only from their fossils. Here is a Pterodactylus fossil.

 ## ROUND 2 **PTERODACTYLUS VS. QUETZALCOATLUS** MATCH 1

Artists can draw what they think pterosaurs looked like, but this is how paleontologists find them. Here is a Quetzalcoatlus fossil.

This is a mismatched battle. The Pterodactylus is the size of the Quetzalcoatlus' head. The Quetzalcoatlus is overpowering. It just flies over to the Pterodactylus and eats it.

QUETZALCOATLUS WINS!

The Rhamphorhynchus had mean-looking teeth. Paleontologists think the Rhamphorhynchus was a fish eater.

FISH FACT
A fish eater is called a piscivore.

PLANT FACT
A plant eater is called a herbivore.

RHAMPHORHYNCHUS VS. TROPEOGNATHUS

The Tropeognathus had teeth. The teeth appear to be perfectly shaped to scoop fish out of the ocean.

BUG EATER FACT
An animal that eats bugs is called an insectivore.

There didn't seem to be any plant-eating pterosaurs.

It's teeth versus teeth. Fish eater versus fish eater. The Tropeognathus is very aggressive. It attacks from above and from below.

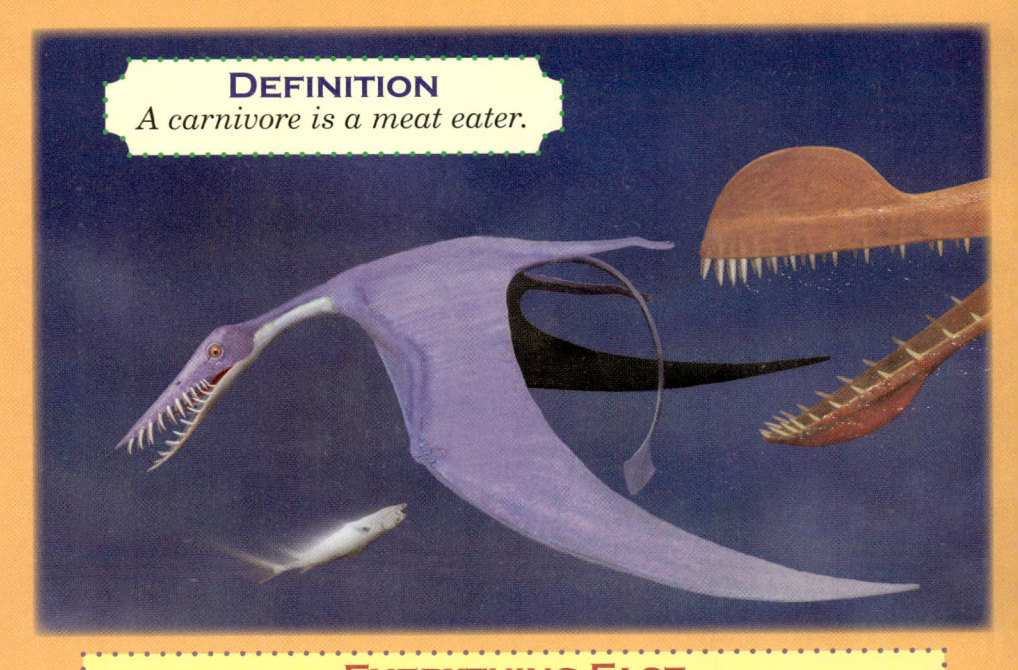

DEFINITION
A carnivore is a meat eater.

EVERYTHING FACT
An animal that eats everything is called an omnivore.

The Rhamphorhynchus puts up a good fight but is eventually defeated.

AUTHOR FACT
The author of this book is an omnivore!

TROPEOGNATHUS WINS!

We will never know what the membrane of a Pteranodon was made of. Maybe some pterosaurs had thicker wings than other pterosaurs. Could the wings have been see-through?

BONE FACT
Pterosaurs had hollow, lightweight bones.

DEFINITION
A membrane is the sheet of skin or leather that forms the wing.

ROUND **2**

PTERANODON VS. ISTIODACTYLUS

MATCH **3**

Were pterosaurs' wings made of skin, like bats' wings?

SEE-THROUGH FACT
Dragonflies, some butterflies, and other insects have transparent, or see-through, wings.

The Istiodactylus has an advantage. It flies near the Pteranodon and blocks the wind. The Pteranodon has to flap its wings harder and harder to try to escape.

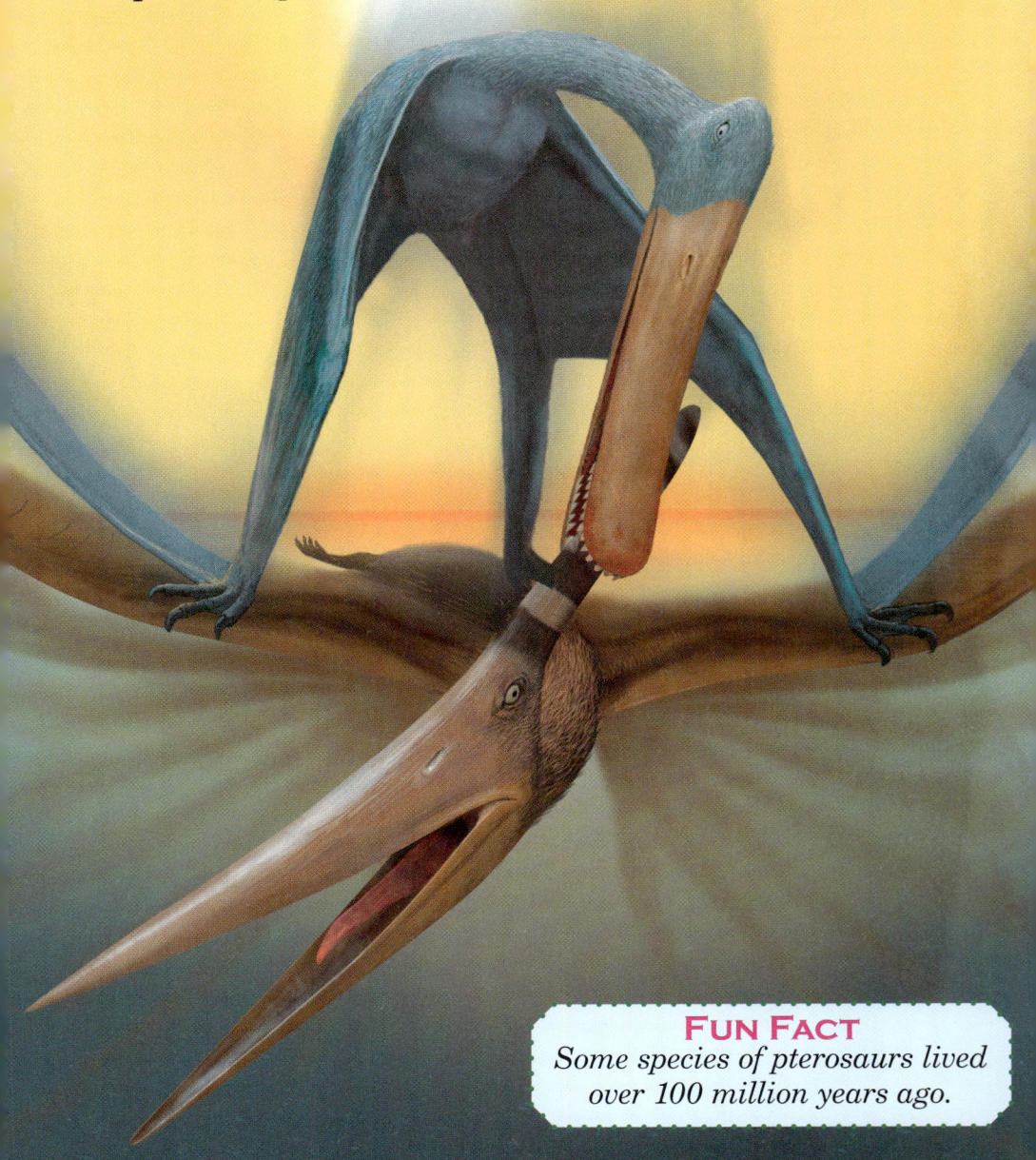

The fight goes on and on. They must have been extra tough. The Istiodactylus eventually sits on the Pteranodon. This forces the Pteranodon down to the ground.

ISTIODACTYLUS WINS!

Here comes a heavyweight match. As we watch this match, think about this: A human has never seen a live pterosaur. A pterosaur never saw a human being. We missed each other by about 65 million years.

ROUND 2

THALASSODROMEUS VS. CRYODRAKON

MATCH 4

The Thalassodromeus has a cute name, but it should not be fighting the giant Cryodrakon. We would love to see the battle between these two. The Thalassodromeus has never seen such a huge, hungry pterosaur.

The Thalassodromeus takes off flying, but the Cryodrakon is faster. It flies up high, but the Cryodrakon can fly higher. It screams and honks loudly, but the Cryodrakon screams and honks louder!

The Cryodrakon bites the wings of the Thalassodromeus. That ends the fight.

CRYODRAKON WINS!

The PTEROSAUR FINAL FOUR is set! It will be the Quetzalcoatlus, Tropeognathus, Istiodactylus, and Cryodrakon.

There are only two matches in round 3. It's the Pterosaur Final Four! We don't know how high pterosaurs could fly. That's because they never told us. Pterosaurs never wrote nonfiction children's books.

PTEROSAUR FINAL FOUR!

ROUND 3 — QUETZALCOATLUS VS. TROPEOGNATHUS — MATCH 1

What do you think? Did pterosaurs fly as high as treetops? Did they fly a mile high? Did pterosaurs prefer to fly over the ocean? Did they prefer to fly over land?

The Tropeognathus is standing on a ledge overlooking the valley. The Quetzalcoatlus is perched on a distant cliff. They both take flight.

The Tropeognathus finds it very difficult to fight the largest known pterosaur. A long battle ensues. The Quetzalcoatlus is too big, too strong, and too skilled for the Tropeognathus.

QUETZALCOATLUS WINS!

On to the finals! Way to go!

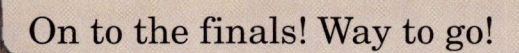

We don't know which was the fastest flying pterosaur. Biggest does not always mean the fastest. Was the Cryodrakon fastest? Was the Istiodactylus fastest?

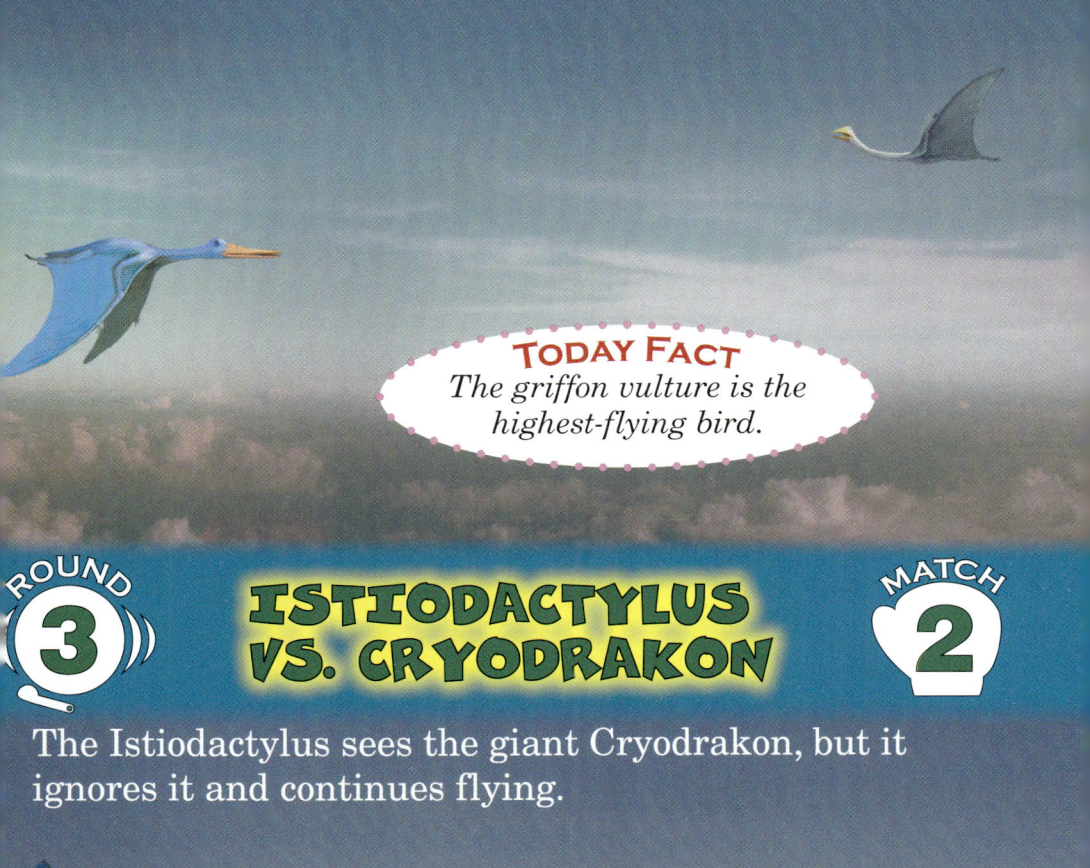

ISTIODACTYLUS VS. CRYODRAKON

The Istiodactylus sees the giant Cryodrakon, but it ignores it and continues flying.

The Cryodrakon changes direction. It flies directly at the Istiodactylus. It's time for a fight! Who will battle the Quetzalcoatlus in the championship match?

The giant shadow of the Cryodrakon intimidates the Istiodactylus. Now the Istiodactylus has lost the will to fight. The Cryodrakon moves in for close-up battle. A bite here and a bite there. The Istiodactylus can no longer fly.

CRYODRAKON WINS!

On to the championship match.

CHAMPIONSHIP MATCH!

This is the matchup the pterosaur fans wanted! These are most likely the two largest pterosaurs that ever flew on Earth.

This championship fight starts in the air. Both pterosaurs get a lift from the updraft of strong winds.

QUETZALCOATLUS VS. CRYODRAKON

The Cryodrakon and the Quetzalcoatlus entangle their wings a few times as their mouths snap at each other.

In the future maybe a fossil hunter will discover a bigger species. For now let these two battle it out.

The fight ends up on the ground. Wow! A ground battle. The Quetzalcoatlus pretends to try to fly. It rushes the Cryodrakon instead and breaks one of its wings. Snap!

QUETZALCOATLUS WINS!

If you wrote your own Pterosaur Rumble, which pterosaurs would you choose? There are more than 150 species to pick from.